I0203244

Written Here:
The Community of Writers
Poetry Review

~ 2013 ~

THE COMMUNITY OF WRITERS AT SQUAW VALLEY

www.communityofwriters.org

Copyright © 2015 Community of Writers at Squaw Valley
ISBN: 978-0-9888953-1-7

All rights reserved. No part of this journal may be reproduced or republished without written consent from the publisher, except by reviewers who may quote brief excerpts in connection with a review in a newspaper, magazine, or electronic pubication; nor may any part of this journal be reproduced, stored in a retrieval system, or transmitted in any form without written consent of the publisher. However, contributors maintain ownership rights of their individual poems and as such retain all rights to publish and republish their work.

Dedicated to

Galway Kinnell

1927 ~ 2014

Founder of the Communty of Writers Poetry Workshop,
with appreciation and gratitude
for his life and poetry, and for his guiding spirit.

TABLE OF CONTENTS 🌿

EDITORS
William Clark
Jennifer C. Humbert
Lori Singer Meyer

DESIGN, TYPESETTING
Liz Thiem

LAYOUT
Amy Rutten

With our deepest thanks to

Forrest Gander, Robert Hass,

Brenda Hillman, Sharon Olds & Evie Shockley,

Staff Poets, 2013

With additional thanks to Larry Ruth.

Written Here: The Community of Writers Poetry Review was printed by LuLu®.

The Poetry Workshop of the Community of Writers is held each summer at Squaw Valley in California's Sierra Nevada. At the workshop, student and staff poets write a new poem each day to be read aloud in the morning session. This gathering of poets, all striving to express ideas, emotions, and concepts, engenders a climate of mutual support, and trust, which makes possible this daily act of courage.

Written Here continues the tradition of publishing poems that first emerged during the summer's Workshop. The poems appearing in these pages were selected by a team of editors, themselves workshop participants, from the work submitted by their fellow poets.

Proceeds from the sales of this anthology benefit
the Poetry Workshop Scholarship Fund.

Kathy Gilbert ~

COMES A SUMMER STORM

White birch glisten, glitter
Rustle and fritter swaying
In a gyre spun

Leaves coquettish as girls
Dancing, flipping skirt hems
Red crinolines underneath,

Pushed to this wanton display
By wind's promise to mist
As it blows through in a sally.

Soft showers flow steady
Beats windows streaked
Morse code dots and dashes.

Umbrella-less, I trudge past
Our Queen of the Snows,
Past workers who upend

Sewer manhole covers, rivet
Inside orange cone space.
I step into the traffic lane

Plug my ears, hope the path
Will be clear around this
Curve of limited visibility.

Larry Ruth ~

MILESTONE CREEK, AUGUST

hiking   all morning   out of Tyndall
through   old trail camps   subalpine meadows

three in line   across the high plateau   lodgepole
     foxtail   whitebark pine

down to the Kern   meander
    and   memory

      heat off granite   warp and weft
streams   of a summers day

climb

    to a river   flowing   of sound

   and water   playing
        tag   with rock

at lunch   waterfall   and sun
   in a canyon   where glaciers retreat

alone

her boots are off   sandals come on
  Máire   wades in

head thrown back   arms reach down
    to the stream   she shakes

       gray   and brown hair is
    a girl again

her fingers
       seine   the water

flows   for a moment
           flows   away

Paul Watsky ~

ERATO TRAFFICKED

Please liberate me from this
collective factory

farm, where I must lay
a poem a day, extra

large, or be pecked
to death by

the flock. Muse
not moo cow, I'm no pea-

brain grafted to hyper-
active ovaries who scram-

bles her skirts above
her waist and bends to

the tupping-*Bull*
or baster, bring

it on! That, brother,
ain't me. I don't perch

on rocks and cackle
about my cleverness, or

revel in perpetual lac-
tation, clamped

by the neck while their mechanical
suck-a-tit drains

my udder. They call this assembly
line a community of

writers, and dose
the feed to rev

production. Afternoons we ab-
sorb motivational

harangues that tout The
Craft (really

about meeting our
quota), such

as "Varieties of Ewe, Forced
Lambing," along with re-

freshers on dropping
one's drafts and amber-

gris: *Cough up, fatty, or
you know what comes*

next. Truth is, nobody's
ever dared to dis-

cover. Please, just smuggle
out my note telling Am-

nesty and PETA where
I'm held, and give them this

feather so they can match poor
Erato's DNA.

Marte Broehm ~

SNOW.

Awake, you are not afraid of snow.
You see it on top of the Sierra Nevadas, marvel at its beauty,
at the crisp-white crystallized on crevices and trapped in
stalled rivulets beneath the precipice.
You stare, swear you can feel the softest of snow at the highest
point hovering near clouds.
You sit on the balcony above a southern edge of Lake Tahoe,
mark each day by the snow-cross on Mt. Tallac...
   how much of it remains...
   how far it reaches north, south, east, west.
You watch its white width melt, miniscule centimeters your eyes
swear they can measure. With your finger, you outline the cross.
You observe its thickness, calculate the ease or difficulty of
ascent...
   how the trail winds from base of the mountain, up.
And you smell *real* air,
feel the thinning of it as you mount higher-and-higher.

> Asleep, you are trapped beneath layers and white,
> snow and ice, flesh turns red, then blue, its cold
> dissolves your skin, an itch and numb to it. You
> know how it wedges and chips, finds a way into
> bone, how it licks warm marrow, sucks at your
> wrists and neck, and marrow lifts into its iced
> mouth. You and the cold. Heavy. The fear of cold.
> Heavy. Snow creates steel beams that hold you, the
> snow holds you beneath its weight, and air burns
> coming into your nose, your mouth. Burns. And
> your lungs clench and burn, fire of cold and ice, its
> merciless sting. So you hold your breath, you close
> your mouth, will your nostrils tight. You hope one
> moment of warmth will come from the burn of
> the freeze, though no warmth comes.

John Briscoe ~

In the Beginning Was What Word?

Venomousness
　　hisses in *Jewess*,
　　　in *Negress*, but it can't be in
　　　　the innate sounds of the words. It must lie
in the sneering sibilating way
　　this man chooses to
　　　　　enunciate them.

　　Then again *mimsy, slithy toves*
and every child's favorite *borogoves*
made us giggle long before Humpty Dumpty
　　　told us and Alice what they meant.
　　　　　For that matter if *borborygmus*
　　were redefined to mean Armegeddon
we'd still titter at its silliness.

　　My grandmother, who raised me, suckled me
　　　she said, would have forbidden me
　　　　to dwell a day in this place,
　　　　Squaw Valley, *squaw* a lower-case crow word
　　　crueler than *digger*, the unutterable,
　　　the for-this-you-fight-son
　D word. I look about, grope, dig hard, for her,
　　but cannot find the hurt.

Ken Haas ~

ON THE LONE PRAIRIE

My father's Jersey grave,
almost grassed over now like its elders—
his parents', in-laws', brother's;
just a wife's berth yet to be filled—
tells me concretely what I've known
only in a thoughtless way:
There's no place for me
in this cleft piecrust of footstones
encircling a granite tongue
blazed with the family name
and cast at heaven.

I was told as a boy,
when he bought just the seven plots,
that the death of one's children
is unthinkable.
But they had already glimpsed
the unthinkable, and I see now
their choice was to draw
a hard round line between
those who had fled and those
for whom the new life had been dreamed,
between the let go and the ones
whose tests were yet to come.

And they were right.
Love notwithstanding, this huddle
in the clenched earth of the East
is not for me.
I want an oven
and burial in capacious air
near my home out West,
smoke arms flung on either side
to make a different pact
with those my family left behind
for me.

Todd Germain ~

FATHER IN TRANSLATION

Never was one for words
or gestures of parting
so that phone held to his ear
you could imagine him hear
your voice, despite his silence.

Spoke, when he spoke, in
Anglo-Saxon roots of English.
Courteously asked, "are you ready to have
        your phlegm suctioned?"
He'd reply, "fuck off."

Found comfort in the language of war.
Described the day's combat:
        doctor knows shit, nurses attack--
                they poke, shoot, pick, push, choke, suck, rip...
Then your battle cry:
        get back up; walk, talk, chew,
                beat this, fight!

Language of medicine baffled.
Told in Latin, "pneumonia," from the Greek
        pneuma (breath), and "bacteria",
            from the Greek bakterion (small staff),
he'd look to you to translate:
        fucked.

And though he may not
hear a word you say,
his substance now beyond your reach,
gone into the breathless abyss
between the sounding of words,
you could imagine him looking
to you, imploring you to make
dying comprehensible,
but how do you translate
the language of unending silence?

Christine Gosnay ~

GATHERED AFTER DUSK

A grudge of April snow falls with Olympic speed
There is at least one thing broken

The moon shakes the stars with its fists where they fly
I lie alone with the ransoms of divorce

The pieces of a porcelain bowl lie about the floor,
open to suggestion as a crocus to radiate frost

One takes the shape of a cloud, which takes
the shape of peace, circle to nothing else

The others break like fools, a cue ball,
a toss of sugar, frisbees, a kindergarten hand,

not different from mine.
I was beautiful as long as my mother was beautiful.

What can you call me now - she slumps over a table
after every meal, thinking about unspooled

cassette tapes, thinking about something all around her,
something as bald and blue as clearing up.

At least one thing is breaking. I will sometime
 have this disease removed, which is only a bit of trouble now.

The old cat, new to duties of comfort, unlaces my legs.
The house rows straight through the sidelong snow.

Lester Graves Lennon ~

LOVE IS TOO DANGEROUS
(for my wife)

Love is too dangerous to be called love
too eagerly when moon-pulled bodies too
easily fit and love songs easily
sung sing from synched star-glazed lips that have sung
before but not together, not before
angels embraced two for their Angelic

Order, dazed them with dazzling wings the Order
replaces quickly while dulled sun replaces
clear night with clouds, lost wings, light rains, the clear
threat of storm heavy weather with lightning threat
slashing perfection's perfumed lyrics, slashing
dreams the rushed night held loosely until dreamers

awake to sleep-caked eyes, their fear awake
calling them apart but not, my love, calling
us loudly enough to call us from us,
angels, if there be angels we are angels,
knowing hard days will still hold moon nights knowing
love is too dangerous not to be love.

Jennifer Humbert ~

TIPS FOR BEAR PROOFING
YOUR HOME

Old Westerns and hotel sheets make the best defense.
Hang em High projected onto garage doors or siding—
guests wrapped like little goblins in high thread counts,
sipping gimlets; bears recoil from such phantasmal excesses.

Bears eat clouds and clover patches, but will settle for pasta.
Store food in anything non-cumulous and wait.
If your kitchen is untouched today, you must protect it again;
wear a sheet shroud and let *True Grit* ring through the night-watch.

Loud crashes encourage bears, brothers to Bacchus that they are,
but whispers attract them even more. Their hearing is poor
and they worry about being made fun of. Their growl and roar
grew as delicate evolutions to protect a winter's worth of feeling.

Naturally curious, bears masquerade as lewd, furry garbage men;
but they wander, poets in the night, looking for material
and star-sanctioned connections. *Paint Your Wagon* plays
tonight so they will slip past your house, unnoticed and alone.

Carl Steen ~

HELPLESS

I am helpless as you are   watching you sleeping
your hands clasped   in special white mittens,
in mesh so your fingers breathe   so your fingers can heal
until jabbed again, for tests   jabbed for white cell counts,
or they will restrain you   to stop you pulling tubes
All I can do is sit bedside   All I can do is wipe dried tears
No talk above a whisper   I must not wake you
All these weeks in this place   The only beauty in this place
Those white mittens and you   you breathing
Your breasts rising and falling   in your gown
Breathing   Breathing   Breathing   Breathing
          Breathing   Breathing   Breathing

Evie Shockley ~

QUESTION MARKS

a woman listens across
an ocean to the sound of her mother's
ageing. it washes up, insistent waves

of unsubpoenaed evidence
lapping—battering—the shore
of her skull, her ear

the conch shell in which the same
mumbled questions break
over and over into foam. sentenced

to pace the subterranean passages
of her mother's mind, she
wonders

whether meaning can survive
this relentless testing.   how do you like
your new house, honey?   so,

how do you like your new house?   how
goes it with your new
house, honey—do you like it?   asked

and asked, as if her feelings
were as flighty as
a murder of crows; as if newness

were a prison-state
the house was locked into, month
upon unmoving month. her job, too,

her husband: each topic a territory,
traveled by a commuter determined
to play the tourist. her sisters:

on the scene, on the clock, on
the double—these conversational
bruises all she can carry

from a distance. through
hollow transatlantic cable, she hears
her mother's voice—   so, honey,

when's your next visit?   can i expect
a visit anytime soon, dear?   now
tell me, honey, when will i

be seeing you?   —and she answers
with facts, then with truths, then with
what should be true.

Lori Singer Meyer ~

LOST AND FOUND

Have you ever thought
how so much of your life
is carved out
from what you missed,
didn't notice, didn't fully attend
like your last decade
shaped from
no doctor asking
if you had been an athlete,
which would have explained
your demanding, I can't breathe!,
even though PEV tests showed
your lung capacity well within normal.

Only last week
did you start breathing again
(diagnosis: asthma)
a doctor ordering
the second line test
frowned at by insurance companies
when first line results are normal,
even though you'd remained bent over,
gasping,
in other doctors' offices.

The outcome:
a twenty percent deficit in lung space
in psychological terms
an enactment
the tennis not played,
soccer not coached,
miles not run along the lake shore,
the person you would marry,
and how you would leave behind

the seemingly perfect job and house
surrounded by a picket fence
somewhere west of Chicago.

Breathe deeply,
pull again
from the lost pile
for the found,
your son's ADHD
prompted the discovery
you couldn't recall
the Krebs cycle in seventh grade
because you needed stimulants;
finding your practice of law
you remember states permitting
third party promissory estoppel
when the judge presses you
on whether your client has a claim.

Breathe deeper,
hold the breath,
feel it hurt before you expel,
take another breath,
one dog is snoring at your feet
the other is pressed close beside your left leg,
each completely unconcerned about his kibble
or whether you will love him in the morning.

Conor Bracken ~

IN APPALACHIA

I climbed a mountain once, and I conquered it.
I was Hannibal finding a pass to elephant through,

and then my father doled out our lunch.
We chewed quietly and passed the water back and forth.

He gazed into the basin of the valley,
and I saw myself in the knolls that nipped the sky,

squat and round, built of unbustable stuff.
I stared at them like they owed my mountain money

and I was the youngest person in the world.
My father knew it; even so he let me lead

the whole way back down the mountain,
back to the lot where we took turns pissing each beside the car

while the other watched for oncoming traffic,
a sudden blare of headlights hacked into the trees

like the white blazes my father watched for,
that marked the trail I thought I was blazing.

Robert Hass ~

STANZAS FOR A SIERRA MORNING

Looking for wildflowers, the white yarrow
With its deep roots for this dry place
And fireweed which likes disturbed ground.

There were lots of them, bright white yarrow
And the fireweed was the brilliant magenta
Some women put on their lips for summer evenings.

The water of the creek ran clear over creekstones
And a pair of dove-white plovers fished the rills
A sandbar made in one of the turning of the creek.

You couldn't have bought the sky's blue.
Not in the silk markets of Samarkand. Not
In any market between Xian and Venice.

Which doesn't mean that it doesn't exist.
Isn't that, after all, what a stanza is for,
So that after a night of listening, unwillingly,

To yourself think, you can walk, slightly hungover,
Through some morning market, sipping tea,
An eye out for that scrap of immaculate azure.

Annie Mascorro ~

FROM 6,000 FEET

"There is no quick, easy, and certain way to distinguish a presumably safe and edible 'mushroom' from an unpalatable or dangerous 'toadstool.'" (From *Sierra Nevada Natural History*)

When my heart reached
two hundred and forty beats
per minute, I thought I would die,
but did not, kept
running just to see. Not thinking of
limits of measure-
ments, nor how
to keep the breath, but of what's
for dinner. Mushrooms. And how once
I spent a summer cutting
morels from a blackened
forest floor, at my side,
 love, every single meal
delicate brown pits, ridged and stuffed.

It is different now. There are more kinds.
Whole books and fields and
how to make a life, to start
again, to tell sulfur shelf from sulpher tuft,
witches' butter from cap of death.

When I call to ask, you pronounce me
alive, advise acclimation-
sleeping in a tent or learning
to fly a small plane. You say to
count the beats out
the old-fashioned way.
Medication is banned, you say,
but time is not.

Jacqueline Hughes Simon ~

The Turtle was 82   Henry Had Owned it His Whole Life

The turtle in the tank   was presumed to have   a charmed life
Saved as it was   from its fate   as turtle soup
Taken from the Chinese woman   who wanted   to eat
Housed in the dining room   with no irony   where the tank fit
Its struggle sounds   like   runoff bouncing
The noise   cups of dice make   as Chinese men
Slap them over   hitting the table with a soft thud   to count their luck

Amy Haddad ~

ANGRY CROW

Shooed away from
my nearly blind mother,
they tell her,
"We're going to get you up now."
For the first time in over a week,
she will stand.
I retreat across the room
to a window that opens on
an abandoned courtyard.
From here I can spy
into other patients' rooms.
I hop up on the window ledge
among packets of IV tubing
and alcohol wipes, back to the view.
I plant my feet on the recliner's arm
ignoring the seat below. I need to be
high enough to see
but I must give space to
those now in charge.
I cant my head and watch them.
My eyes bright with mistrust,
I am ready to swoop down
if she needs me,
when they need me. They push and
cajole, prodding her upright
but she cannot catch their soft voices
without her hearing aids
lost somewhere in the linens. I repeat
what they say, shouting from my perch.
They tell me to be quiet
so they can do their job. She hangs
between them head down but
the trick isn't over
until she raises her head.
She looks up for a second
then begs to lie down
asking them where I have gone.

Lisa L. Moore ~

ALBERTA FLOODS

Thirteen thousand
evacuated from High River,
the Dairy Queen where we took her
from the Home for her weekly cone not even a dimple
in the lapping flood. The Highwood River has overflowed its banks.

Glacial meltwater, our swimming hole, the river was never safe.
Even in August it numbed
the feet after a few minutes. We jumped in
upstream so the water
could hurl us, furious, as far as the flat beach
beside the barn.
My brother clung blue and puking to the canoe in lieu of learning

to swim.
That last summer,
vowing never again, I lay
on the hot, flat sandstone hoping
to brown my skin, shed something, melt
some ease into in my chest. I am homesick
for those mountains, where I never was at home. Tic tac toe
scratched onto the flat rock washed away now. All my rivers are in flood.

Cameron Jackson ~

SPILL SPILLING
STILL

a roller coaster seen from the freeway
ridden in the dream, through the dream
with the dream or as the dream
beginning between two memories
of August-- a yellow white wheatfield
and deep sky deep water blue

the dream like timeriver in the clouds
or frozen into shapes, colored by the heat
of their melting, deep flowing underground
beneath many layers of black and brown

silver shards of mirror stuck into the sand,
shining, because the memory of the dream
is not the dream
                    I've stopped seeing the
difference between ghosts and trees, between
mirrors and me, I am everywhere Narcissus
colored by my heat the wheatfields of August
remembering future memories of dreams
asking them where I have gone.

Peter Schireson ~

A Chinese Fan and The Wind

We commandeered a boat,
then we jumped into the sea
and swam with no end to the water,
sank the boat, leaped into the sky,
and flew with no end to the air.

We were swimming, water, flying,
and air. But we weren't fishes or birds.

We found a place without
a sea, or air, or boats. Or anything
else. A place that just had us.
And wood. We built a fire
with the wood and filmed it while
it turned to ash and watched to see
if you or I could tell exactly
when it turned.

I'd been wood before,
so you were the wood
and I was the ash.

We climbed a mountain
where it was always windy,
made a Chinese fan and fanned
ourselves in the wind so the wind
could see we were swimming, water, flying,
and air, you the wood and the bird,
and me the fish and the ash.

I was the Chinese fan
and you were the wind.

Monica Minott ~

CASUALTIES OF WAR

Iraq Body Count: 174,000 civilian and combat deaths
Iraq Lancet Survey: 601,027 voilent deaths
Opinion Research: 1,033,000 deaths as a result of conflict in Iraq.

Is it enough for me to plant red ginger,
        to ask questions firemongers can't answer?
        Questions spawning more questions.
          There is no parting the Sea of Reeds.

The water table rising, nothing comes of it.
        Your will for me? Creeping desolation, potent,
        imagined weapons of mass destruction.
          the balancing force of the dead, their redress.

I need not put on the blood red dress of Marcu Crassus
        having defeated Spartacus,
        nor will I tie you to me with fear.
          Global warming is shock and awe enough.

Now, the halo of fire will descend

        will sit, will break into tongues,

        will visit the heads of firemongers,

        constructs of leaders...exposed.

As to the meaning of the bloody statistics?
        Nothing comes to it.
        Nothing leaves it.

Curt Last ~

PASHTO

Inpatient Ward has three wards, two of which are for local patients.
I pick up small words and phrases by watching the other corpsmen
and interacting with the interpreters and locals during direct care:

Manana—"Thank you."
Whenever I finish taking care of a patient or working with the relative of
a child patient, I make it a point to say this. I also say it to the interpreters after I've asked them
for assistance during patient work ups. Courtesy is a working universal.

Portiko—"Up."
Used when patient movement is deliberate, such as during linen change, or
having a restless, semi-conscious Afghani strapped to their bed so they don't fall out, or pull out
their IV lines or ECG leads. Often they have to be moved up from slumping.

Ola Klassika—"Open your mouth."
Probably the second most utilized phrase, as when we take
vitals, we have to get a temp with a thermometer. Also used when administering oral meds to
Afghanis who have had their eyes blown out or destroyed by an IED blast.

Tajiman—"Interpreter."
First time I heard this phrase, a detainee was yelling it. I thought he was
calling out to one of his dead buddies, until the interpreter came in and educated me. The ANA,
ANP, and civilian locals in Ward 3 yell this all day long while in pain.

Dawa—"Medicine."
I should include a question mark after that, since we always have to ask the
Afghanis in Ward 3 if they need meds—but only within physician-directed scheduling, since
these guys always seem to say "yes" or constantly ask for pain meds.

Darkee—"Pain."
A word more compelling than 'love,' as everyone's actually felt it.
Often combined with *dawa*, as in *Darkee dawa?* ("Do you need pain meds?"). Again,
used sparingly, as many locals smoke opium, and have a low pain tolerance as a result.

This is about all of the Pashto I know, and probably will ever know.

26

Anna Ross ~

Self-Portrait With Geography

In the locker room at the community pool,
my daughter, skinny-limbed in her blue
and lime green swimsuit, measures herself
to my shoulder, then presses one sharp finger
into the loose skin below my navel,
laughing to see the white indented moon
she leaves there.

> From high enough, one body
> looks like any other —10-year-old girl
> collecting firewood or man with gun —
> the coordinates close and closing.

From the pool's deck, I watch her kick
and bob in chlorine blue,
torso and legs a momentary T
against the black spine of the lane
wavering beneath.

> *...solely with the intent of countering known*
> *insurgents,*
> the NATO spokesman speaks
> in Laghman Province, Afghanistan.
> Her body bends—a piece of white cloth
> fluttering—
> then straightens holding a stick.

In the pool, she rolls and thrashes—
element within element—elbow
flashing in air before it falls beneath
then reappears—*Watch me!*

Is this a day she's waited for, old enough now
to work, the women with their bundles—
aunts, the cousin married this spring,
grandmother—
nodding to her in the beginning light
of the hour before the early walk to school
(Is there a school?), collected brush stacked
neatly
as the planes *engage with precision munitions*
and direct fire.

hip, flank,
shoulder at the water's lip—*Watch...I'm—*
white flutter kick above the center line—
An arm crooks out, fingers splayed,
each tendon raised and seeking
as she reaches for the wall.

Or would she have slept,
small moon beneath her blanket—
Unfortunately, we have become aware of possible
civilians—let someone else
walk into still dark morning,
someone else
search out the branches to burn that hour.

Forrest Gander ~

EQUAL TO THESE FLOWERS

Such moments he marks,
recalling them to his son—as when
they sledded Suicide Hill and spilled
from the sled, the boy landing on top
of his father who slid in his slick down
jacket down the hill on his back
clutching his son, the both of them
wheezing with laughter—
freeze into set pieces through the father's
reportage and are finally, for him, far
less affecting than what
goes unmeasured and floats
around him with motes
of dust. Ordinary and unsorted.

Diana Khoi Nguyen ~

THE KARAKUL OF KURDISTAN

We stood in the sparse highland of a desert,
wearing salt from a fog that came lightly.
A seed laid buried in the mountain, beating.
The wingbeat of moths drowned in the fog.

You had the feeling you were blocking
your own way simply by being.
Like a cat bringing a dead bird to the base of an oak.
Except the bird was your heart.

We are not the kind of creature to carry tales.
Dust floats from the yarrow into our wool.
The newborns from their coats fly into coal.
And from the coals, heat burns dirt to our hooves.

We shall never know why
all change involves a death, but you do.
A man in felted slippers who discovers illness
feels in him a sweetness keen as pain.

Sheep are not only sheep in this desert.
Deep fright at your own smallness stops you,
slowly, with the relish of a farmhand.
Your hands like dirty sparrow talons: trembling.

Sometimes you dream you are your own son.
We graze and lambs graze within us.
Dark comes on, then rain, but nothing is certain.
It is not an animal choice to refrain from killing.

Emma Estrella ~

WAITING IN THE ARMS ROOM

nervous, they drink beer,
eat cold pizza, wait—
the hours endless,
like the months before.

the air conditioning throbs
against the georgia heat
that lurks around
the old army structure,
looking to get inside.
someone has turned the radio on;
no one is listening.

so many women, all ages,
some so pregnant
they can barely hoist their bodies
from the plastic chairs
to check, with the others,
when they hear what sounds
like a bus coming down
the inscrutable drive—
down from the airfield
down from the airplane
down from the sky
that bridges this world
with the one they're
waiting on—

finally there really is
an engine rumbling
in the southern dusk
and they all rush out,
stand silent,
waiting for husbands
          who will never entirely
          return.

31

Pamela Sue Hitchcock ~

THE SQUID

Devoured by woods, by the squid-
like willows where I hid to read,
there is more ferocity

in spring than war. Here is no longer a tree—
it has gone to make the beekeeper's

table.
I am archetypal,

  leper,
but the squid, she moves,
searching water.

Will Clark ~

THE DIPLOMAT

The veins of our greatest longing,
scions of our most ill-defined wealth
elastic with intention and design,

sculpt themselves into factious truths,
root themselves into sticky tents,
and nest themselves with such ease,

ruling with their impulse to clasp.
What they touch singes their thinnest
sensitive hairs, and we are glad.

Sheila Davies Sumner ~

THE PAROLE BOARD IN CUBISM

". . . though people are often murdered, to celebrate the death of love."
- Sharon Olds, *Stags Leap*

In a murderer's hands the beloved lives — sure.
Blood content, a crocus — (I heard.)
When alive we're — yeah — she's
in the eyes & fingers of the universe — agreed — beheld.

Panel of people with moral fibers, the direction they naturally lie.
A Hearing Examiner — a wet recording — an offender present.
In the theatre of human absence that aims to be the new tomorrow
a single ballerina, en pointe — is she the? — hops on one foot off her horse
power — executes a Pas de cheval
Pas de cheval

The hills are purple and hurt — aren't they?
And god our tired aerialist.
Mercury — quick — — Attitude — step step up
Hermes — winged Sandals
and over, a little river. Staff

They execute, shooting
a flying Brisé Volé shattered while flying seesaw through — beaten into pigeons — the air
But these valley mountains of indigenous awe inflect an early snow
suit fluid red —

— sweep — back in a body line.

Backhand her soul over the dun green ballad
mortality hound howling

and what does a murderer do — blood on hand — with a soul
riding an eclipse of life?

(I see us kin crushed by — of course — on the south edge of this document.)

You may enter the registry only
through this small gate at the back of your soul, resting
state of humanity — immortal.

laughter

34

Martha Yates ~

THE VINEYARDS OF NAPA

Vine stanchions carve
green hillsides into white
diagonals running up the slopes
and over the side to the war
cemetery at Yountville.

> *Pvt. Franklin Baker died for the Union*
> *at Antietam, Captain Nathan Brown*
> *died on Utah Beach.*

Pinot Noir, the Blanc, the Blue,
the Beaujolais -- grapes gorge
themselves and bloat -- plucked packed
in boxes taken for crushing, to ferment
till their spirits rise.

The headstones
in perfect alignment of white
diagonals of the dead,
their engraved letters, shadows
in stone slabs.

> *Corporal Daniel Joy died at Da Nang,*
> *Colonel Jonathan Todmann at Verdun,*
> *Sgt. James Conwell at Bagram.*

The poet wrote, *"Grapes feed on light."*
We too feed -- out of the canker
of the many dead, out of the sickness
of recurring war -- do these dead rise
in some other form?

Sawnie Morris ~

INLAND SEE

re: "Deepwater Horizon" catastrophic oil spill, June 2010

Grandmothers scoop up a light-net,
haul pelican (in the spirit world) like fish —
and fish. Or net the sludge,
thick ooze, and how-to
staunch a puncture. (Sometimes
we must protect ourselves, we said of television,
internet.) Our fingers
over dinner, splay—were we? Eating a bird,
we become it.

Amy Pence ~

BAYOU GHOST TREES

Rough planks over the swamps at Barataria   century-old bald cypresses rise from

        brackish the water

           the day crafty with scent

Jean Lafitte   waits to re-emerge   *by all accounts a handsome man*

      calls himself a privateer   *never*

                say pirate to his face

      wet leaves mulch   insects work   soil

          turns body's flesh   effigy   into sand

Barataria   *all the lakees*   *swamps*   *bays south of New Orleans*

    Gulf of Mexico

        Grand Isle   *Grande Terre*

Fall light   apricots   the bayou

        a pseudo-acacia

     suspends her seed pods—

Pirates infiltrate   *myriad bayous*   *all the way to New Orleans*

    impossible to patrol

      Was there a tear in the portal?   Were you   Grandmother

    quite near?

        By 2050, with no intervention   *Grand Terre will   disappear*

Dusk   creatures arrive

        gator   shifts   night's shroud   body

   secretes   *the birthplace of the Lafittes*

   could be Port-au-Prince   *San Domingo*   *Bayonne, France*

Grandmother   looks out

                a window   dying

mouths lap backward   into some majestic sleep

             as in some tether—

      Hurricane winds favored   *bald cypress*   *water tupelo*

button bush   a tear in night's —   what form would

        it take?

the bodies, after the hurricane, putrefy   *sink then rise*

           Over the swamp's muddy listen   seed

pods suspend   withered forms of men

    smuggling   *contraband, luxuries*   *or slaves*   *legends of Lafitte*

    flourish   *King Arthur / Robin Hood*

    Sway the leaves, Grandmother   saturate

              the landscape

           seeds   their in-dwelling

holding   being's many forms

      atoms   the void—   whether

              to be human

Kathi Stafford ~

GRANDMOTHER JEWELL

A house could be under construction—
   pour the slab, throw up the walls, build
         a roof, plaster the interior, plumb the place.

Here in the middle of this forest
   a home where we could drink
         mint tea from a thin cracked pot.

Always use your best china.
   The lesson my grandmother
         taught me summer after summer.

It's a trick to build well
from a wobbly start.

This woman wore red wigs
   and constructed her face each day
         with cosmetics shipped from France.

Shaped her brows with care and precision. Wore
   baby blue silk dresses, covered
         with dragonflies in mid-flight.

Jewell's time came and went. My cousins
   never cared for her much but I was
         the favorite girl, always looking

At shots of her with Indira Gandhi in Bombay
   while she fed me cold plums and
         peanut butter ice cream.

She had her secrets, including a blank
    wedding license we found after she passed,
        but she wouldn't want that known

Any more than those three wig stands
    sporting fake auburn gleam, stiff and rough,
        that stood sentinel by the bed.

Ann Fisher-Wirth ~

BUTOH

> *You must either watch a fire or burn up in it.*
> *--attributed (perhaps) to William Faulkner*

When I told M. about my fascination
                    with butoh, she said, "Living
        as you do,   .
                with a formal job, in a
formal life,
                it makes sense you'd be drawn
                            to the shape of a body
                    writhing."

You are flinging me about
                                    like a branch
                    in the wind, aren't you?
        A branch that whips
and flails and its
                ragged petals are sodden
                        with rain, rain-translucent

                and plastered against
        the leaves.
                    Yet it just wants
                        more, more, more—
                    more being shaken, to be broken.
"What happens if you break?" asks M.

        God's dancer, tongues of fire,
how did I ever get born
                    in middle America?

What language in me but fucking
                    says, "I know you, river.
I bow to you, sun"? Only then
            does my tongue
                        shoot forth and my jaw
                freeze over, only then
do I acknowledge
        what the universe was made for.

            There's no tradition of craziness
                            for me, no ritual
                    of release; my ancestors
            sit in their chairs
when they listen to music.

Cynthia Arrieu-King ~

COMPANION SILENCE

Lithe morning gone   lights dimming
the little girl knocking her ball by my feet
looks into my face
and flees—
           Sunday, I cannot
make you so full of work. The electric bill stays

in my purse, though they are open 24 7 & I've paid
for power in a place I haven't lived for a month.

This is fixable. I hear no one likes you much,
they dread work, they cite the melancholy,

the ones who don't have to drive the late shuttle
or plank out dozens of tan bottles on a shelf, serve,

but still there's your drawing down
jellyfish evenly suspended, drifting in a tank.

So many winters, the dread of 5:30PM Mass
late Sunday—last chance for lazybones—

red velvet, a heavy nod, words breaking,
the incense and censer. The deep wish

for each part to be over. The bleeding
stained glass going black. Censer

tipping out ash. A hallowed space,
the place to be but distractedly, the way

holding a letter in steam or drawing a bowl
through clean water works. Fumes. Balms.

Then, at home, self-balms. A worry, minor
key, dissolves. Plates clatter. Travel allows

you to think what you really mean, dream
the mannequins-on-turntable dreams,

a colleague suddenly rubbing your back;
an afternoon stripped away to wild or to needed.

Meara Sharma ~

ON ELLIOT'S BEACH, CHENNAI (HALF-MOON)

eight years later, the beach is wide again, glowing
on this blue night. the sand undulates. below,
crabs build delicate, interlocking homes.

the materials out of which the shore is made
have dissolved. the wooden boats, the barrels,
the armchairs, the umbrellas, the kerosene lamps,
the car bodies, the tarpaulins, the radios,
the school uniforms, the cast-iron pots,
the pencils, the knives, the bones.

a woman draped in iridescent green rises
from a misshapen pile on the fine sand. dirt
encrusts her skin-bound limbs but her face
is arrestingly precise. she drinks the light
of the moon and behind her blanketed
bodies stir, as if satiated.

it is unkind to look. but I long to touch this
beautiful fleshless woman, to inhabit her
concave figure and yoke her shorn nerves
to mine. someone must unfurl her pain and I
am exorbitantly alive.

the wind lifts the sand into the air. and
I wonder whether empathy needs organs
to survive, whether these eggshell bodies
share some frequency, some reverberating air
with those seven boys in Syria, licking dew
off the walls of a cave, expecting
their mother to return.

45

what is the latitude of suffering?
when the ground hiccupped
he spilled the freshly boiled milk
meant for yogurt. she screamed
and then the news came. a wave
had swept its muscular tongue
across the lip of the city with such

force that it crumbled, irrevocable,
into the churning bulge of the sea.

Flower Conroy ~

HEART IMPALED

Take these nothing tokens. Think tarot card—seven of swords
predicting the future perfect—or drowsy long-throated
birds, swans or loons
or flamingos dropped from the sky
into a poppy field because that is what the mind entangled
in dream craves. Image lifted from history or the macabre
of religion, as in: I take
upon my tongue
the word, this body. Wholly swallow.
I am the reduction of when they tuck away
their stemnecks. How they seem tufts stuck to a gash,
dusk-bludgeoned clouds staining the cave's wall,
the opposite of bloodsmatter on newly welt
snow. The beating, after-
wards—meaning, its silence. You are the redreamed
hunter & I *won't*—until I break—salt & rose-
mary rubbed, the heart spit-through, roasts
over a firepit chambered in the thin woods where
I dream you. Babydoll
dress, underwear, barefoot, my Timber-
lands by the door. The blinding simultaneous suns,
one hiding the other, from the rubble cathedral: organ music
so that my fern tongue unfurls. Quick lick of claret—
the hunter's fingers—seed, pulse
measure, erasure.

David Watts ~

The Delicate Sprigs of Love

He is sitting next to her.
The firmness of her thigh is pressed against his.
There is no light between them.

He listens so heavily
into the heartbeat of her that he hears the murmuring
of aspens on the hillside.

He tells her this.
How could he sit next to her if he didn't
tell her this?

She is beautiful
in the manner in which there is so much beauty
it almost cancels itself.

I can lie down
in the golden shape of your shadow, he says,
and no longer question myself.

She wonders
if they were just prisoners of the freedom
that brought them there.

Or if to love him
would mean waiting for promises, lying awake,
in the draft of crossing stars.

They kiss
and though he is still alone in the fear that no one will ever kiss him
he is sitting next to her.

Heather Dobbins ~

SHANTYFOLK DANCE FLOOR
the shanty preacher's daughter

I'll pick a shantyman over anybody to dance with.
Hips and stories in fever, sweat and meeting.

I saw him at a shoreline café. The fried fish, spent.
All the rolls ate up. Set our mouths to crave music and moon.

He asked, *You want to watch something die?*
We dancing right now, full up.
Snatch a fish from Red River and toss it in the Mississippi

or turn its head downstream. Our shoes and pine floor, the music
in scuffle then reed. He said, *You can have a doughball with a blink*
of garlic, even the bait Black-tie Tom— Who? *gave you, but no greedy*

fish will bite after a moon you can count by, too gorged on light.
I told him I was counting on him, didn't need a line just a good pole.
Got to eat, woman. Then let us partake. The saxophone's song was wet.

He never said my name after we were introduced.
I wasn't playing at Lady. Our bodies were pressed, a two-fingered note.

The second night, he said, *That dog you love most—*I don't have a—
Your best hunter of muskrat and possom. Possom too ugly to eat.
The one who could paw his path up a twisted trunk but is now an old mess.

Like that drummer there, looking like a pile of sacks
a roustabout wouldn't wear? *Leave him sleep on Spanish moss— the sickening*
quick, a mercy. I said, Should've been a bitch there.

Law does not govern the river. We can go without sight but not sound.
A true river man knows how to lean, to move with and against.

I closed his eyes with my lips. Time to call. Time to respond.
I was current he could hold.

Hillary Katz ~

Nightfall

On the first night, steam rises from the lake. The distance
between us is measured in mosquitoes. The bats wake up,
skim the sky like shadows. The day empties of its visible madness:

the air loses its heaviness, the moth trapped in the cabin stops
beating itself against the screen. We stare into the fire until
our faces appear in the flames. I jump in the lake only when

the sun fully sets because it's easier not knowing what I'm
deep into. I tell you I like to watch up-close the ripples turn
silver with moonlight. That in dark water my body feels like

a beginning. Really, when small waves slosh against themselves
I think of a car filling and sinking. When minnows flutter against
my stomach it's like the ghost of a child blowing streams and streams

of bubbles. Later, when the fire has gone out, you reach to touch me
and I slip away from you like an uncaught fish. When I go to get
a glass for water, the only ones I can reach are covered in dust.

Timothy Dyke ~

ODE TO SHAME

In the hot tub my foamy nude friend says I love you
I say I love you too   and he says
          I didn't say I love you   I said
I love youtube
who writes about love writes about that black shadow
on the mid-day mountain
                              drop
                    I expect to see the gondola
                    I cannot see the gondola
I am a small man trapped in the body of a large man
I am the hulking dude with the neck tattoo
                                   who will not kick your ass

I don't miss the summer I came down from Ecstasy in Vermont flower fields
                              I miss my naive certainty that
spiritual epiphany rounded every bend

who writes about love writes about shame who writes
about God writes about shame who writes about nature
writes about shame who writes about sex writes about
shame you are my best drug
                         shame you are my slippery skin
wet sheet shame
bed bug shame
                    whispers for screens   body made of windows
   Shame you are the caterpillar that must be passed through
Metaphor of corridors
Shame you are my dry cocoon

Meryl Natchez ~

The Ways I See You

the flash of the hook
when I rise to the bait

      how your eyebrows give the joke away

in your baseball cap
and championship t-shirt

      the mean set your mouth can take

talking to yourself
on the treadmill at the gym

      your willingness to try even swing-dance, even yoga

full black beard
pounding abalone

      gray stubble and no particular place to go

in a suit with a mike
at our daughter's wedding

      your shoulder against a dolly under something heavy

on I-5, on 880
talking, missing the exit

      the current I stand in, its surge and drag

your hands over the sink
on the keyboard
with hammer or exacto or pen

      your face in the mirror next to mine

day after day forgetting to really look at you
as if you would be here forever

      so deep
           that hook

CONTRIBUTORS

CYNTHIA ARRIEU-KING works as an associate professor of creative writing at the Richard Stockton College of New Jersey and a former Kundiman fellow. She is the author of two collections of poetry, *People are Tiny in Paintings of China* (2010) and *Manifest* (2013). She also co-wrote a chapbook with Ariana-Sophia Kartsonis, *By a Year Lousy with Meteors* (2013).

CONOR BRACKEN's work has been nominated for the *Best of the Net*, and appears or is forthcoming in *Handsome, Harpur Palate, the minnesota review, Puerto del Sol,* and others. He received his MFA from the University of Houston, where he was a poetry editor for *Gulf Coast*.

JOHN BRISCOE has been a longshoreman, a lawyer, a journalist, teacher and poet. His published works include books on history, law, and one slim volume of poetry. He has tried and argued cases before the Supreme Court of the United States and the Permanent Court of Arbitration in The Hague, and has served as Special Adviser to the United Nations on the environmental consequences of war. He is a Distinguished Senior Visiting Scholar at the University of California Berkeley, and adjunct professor at UC Hastings College of the Law. He writes poetry, some of which is humorous, a bit of which intentionally so.

MARTE BROEHM's poems and prose mingle images across subject matter and regional location. Her work has appeared in *Los Angeles Review, Arsenic Lobster, Hummingbird Review, Magee Park Poets, Pedestal Magazine, Perigee Literature for the Arts, San Diego Poetry Annual,* and elsewhere. She co-facilitates Ponto Beach Poets, a poetry workshop each summer. Watercolors and mixed media pieces exhibit in local galleries. Marte lives in Escondido, CA.

FLOWER CONROY is the author of two chapbooks, *Escape to Nowhere,* and the forthcoming *Controlled Burn*. She earned her MFA from Fairleigh Dickinson University. Her poetry has appeared in *American Literary Review, Poydras Review, Menacing Hedge,* and other journals. She currently lives in Key West.

WILLIAM CLARK recently graduated with an MFA in Creative Writing from the University of Texas in Austin where he served as poetry editor for *Bat City Review*. His work can be found in *Clade Song, smoking glue gun, Iconograph Magazine, California Northern,* and *Berkeley Poetry Review*. In 2005, he was the recipient of an artist residence grant from the Helene Wurlitzer Foundation. He teaches writing at the College of San Mateo.

HEATHER DOBBINS's poems and reviews have been published in *Beloit Poetry Journal, Big Muddy, The Rumpus, The Southern Poetry Anthology* (Tennessee), and *TriQuarterly Review*, among others. Her book of poems, *In the Low Houses*, was published in March 2014 by Kelsay Press. She currently resides in her hometown of Memphis. www.heatherdobbins.com.

TIMOTHY DYKE has published fiction and poetry in *Santa Monica Review, Drunken Boat, Kugelmass, Spork*, and other publications. He has an MFA from the University of Arizona and currently teaches high school students in Honolulu, Hawaii where he lives with three parrots.

EMMA ESTRELLA is a California poet, born and raised in Steinbeck's Salinas Valley, and a recent graduate of UC Davis' Creative Writing MA program. Estrella's recent work focuses on the personal sacrifices of war and the struggle to reacclimate to civilian life. She lives with her husband in Sacramento, CA.

ANN FISHER-WIRTH's most recent books of poems are *Dream Cabinet* (Wings 2012) and *Carta Marina* (Wings 2009). She is coeditor with Laura-Gray Street of *The Ecopoetry Anthology* (Trinity UP 2013), a ground-breaking collection of American ecopoetry with an introduction by Robert Hass. She teaches at the University of Mississippi and directs the Environmental Studies minor; also she teaches yoga at Southern Star in Oxford.

FORREST GANDER, a writer and translator with degrees in geology and English literature, was born in the Mojave Desert and grew up in Virginia. Among his most recent books are the novel *The Trace*, the poems *Eiko & Koma*, and two anthologies: *Panic Cure: Poetry from Spain for the 21st Century* and *Pinholes in the Night: Essential Poems from Latin America*. Gander's book, *Core Samples from the World*, was a finalist for the Pulitzer Prize and the National Book Critics Circle Award. He was a returning faculty member at the Poetry Workshop in 2013.

TODD GERMAIN is a child psychotherapist in private practice in Manhattan, where he lives with his wife and two children to whom he is grateful for bravely holding down the fort while he was out at Squaw Valley. Todd has been writing poetry for over 30 years and has enjoyed participating in classes and workshops with Sharon Olds, Galway Kinnel, Allen Ginsburg, David Trinidad, and others.

KATHY GILBERT received an MFA in Creative Writing from San Francisco State in 2013 after working for thirty-two years in the Bay Area's public transportation sector. Barely published, she writes poetry, memoir, fiction and ten minute plays. When not scribbling she swims, does tai chi and tutors third graders in reading. Her son Eli, age 30, lives with her in Daly City.

CHRISTINE GOSNAY is the founding editor of *The Cossack Review*. Her poetry and essays appear in *POETRY, Sugar House Review, Juked, DIAGRAM, THRUSH Poetry Journal, Vol. 1 Brooklyn*, and other publications. She lives in California.

KEN HAAS lives in San Francisco, where he works in healthcare and sponsors a poetry writing program at the UCSF Children's Hospital. His poems have appeared in *Alabama Literary Review, Caesura, The Cape Rock, Freshwater, Helix, Natural Bridge, Quiddity, Red Wheelbarrow, Schuylkill Valley Journal, Stickman Review, Tattoo Highway*, and *Wild Violet*, and have been anthologized in *The Place That Inhabits Us* (Sixteen Rivers Press, 2010).

AMY HADDAD is the Director, Center for Health Policy & Ethics and the Dr. C.C. and Mabel L. Criss Endowed Chair in the Health Sciences at Creighton University. Her publications include numerous journal articles and chapters, several books, and a film based on the legacy of nursing ethics. Her poetry has been published in the *American Journal of Nursing, Fetishes: Literary Journal of Colorado Health Sciences Center, Journal of Medical Humanities, Touch, Janus Head, Ars Medica*, and the *Bellevue Literary Review.*

ROBERT HASS is a poet, translator, and essayist. He has authored many books of poetry, including *Time and Materials*, which was awarded the Pulitzer Prize and the National Book Award in 2007. He served as Poet Laureate of the United States from 1995 to 1997. Awarded a MacArthur Fellowship and the National Book Critics Circle Award twice, as well as the 2014 Wallace Stevens Award, he is a professor of English at UC Berkeley and directs the Poetry Program of the Community of Writers at Squaw Valley.

PAMELA HITCHCOCK is a student at the University of Arkansas, Fayetteville, where she studies German, creative writing, and translation. Though a native of Tahlequah, Oklahoma, she has lived in the Ozark Mountains of Arkansas since 1987.

JENNIFER HUMBERT received her MFA from Emerson College in 2011; since then, she worked as an adjunct instructor for a few years and now works for a Boston-based start-up. After a few exciting years in Missouri (no, seriously!) she lives in Chicago with her family, where she writes and enjoys walking/biking everywhere.

CAMERON JACKSON is a poet, curator, and opera librettist. In 2009 he and fiancé Jessica Cox cofounded and directed the Alphonse Berber Gallery in Berkeley and later Alphonse Berber Projects in San Francisco. He now lives in Portland, Oregon where he attends the low residency Fiction program at Pacific.

HILLARY KATZ's poems have appeared in *Salamander, burntdistrict, A cappella Zoo, Rufous City Review*, and other journals. She is an editorial assistant for *Weave Magazine*. Originally from Vermont, she now lives in San Francisco and teaches elementary school.

CURT LAST lives in Huntington Beach, California. He earned his Bachelor's Degree in Pre-Law from the University of California, Santa Barbara and his Master of Fine Arts in Poetry from California State University, Long Beach. He is currently serving as a Hospital Corpsman in the United States Naval Reserves. Duties have included a humanitarian mission to East Timor and a deployment to the Role 3 Combat Hospital in Kandahar, Afghanistan.

LESTER GRAVES LENNON's has two published books of poetry, including *The Upward Curve of Earth and Heavens* (2002) and *My Father Was A Poet*, which was published in 2013. Mr. Lennon is an investment banker who lives with his family in the Los Angeles megalopolis where he is a member of the Los Angeles Poet Laureate Task Force. He also serves on the advisory board of the West Chester University Poetry Center and the English Department of the University of Wisconsin, and on the Board of Directors of the Community of Writers at Squaw Valley.

ANNIE MASCORRO received an MFA in poetry from *The University of Montana*. Her poetry and essays have appeared in *Calyx, Epilepsy U.S.A., WorldView Magazine, Montana Public Radio's Collegium Medicum, Sixfold, Ostrich Review, Pudding Magazine*, and *ZYZZYVA*. She is the recipient of the 2007 *Five Fingers Review* Poetry Prize. She lives in Auburn, CA where she is a psychiatric nurse, poetry instructor, and poetry therapist in training.

LORI SINGER MEYER is a full-time mom, and sometime lawyer and poet. Mom of a wonderful nine-year-old son, Samuel, she has returned to writing poetry after a long hiatus. She currently resides in McLean, VA, with Samuel, three dogs, and a cat - her horse is in Middleburg, VA.

MONICA MINOTT is a Chartered Accountant. She received two awards in the Jamaican National Book Development Council's annual literary competitions for book-length collections of her poetry. She was awarded first prize in the inaugural Small Axe poetry competition. Her poems have been published in the *Caribbean Writer* and *Small Axe*, and the *Jubilation Anthology*. Poems have been aired on *Power 106, Jamaica* and a Sacramento, California radio station.

LISA L. MOORE's writing has been awarded the Lambda Literary Foundation Award and the Art/Lines Juried Poetry Prize. She is the author or editor of four scholarly books and her poems have appeared in journals and anthologies including *Lavender Review, Sinister Wisdom,* and *Broadsided.* She is Professor of English at The University of Texas at Austin.

SAWNIE MORRIS won the 2010 PSA Bogin Memorial Award for a selection of 5 poems and has been co-winner of the New Mexico Book Award for her chapbook in *The Sound a Raven Makes* (Tres Chicas Books, 2006). Her poems have appeared in *Denver Quarterly, drunkenboat.com, The Journal,* and other magazines. Her writing about poetry has appeared in *The Kenyon Review, Contemporary Literary Criticism,* and *Boston Review.*

MERYL NATCHEZ took a leave of absence from college in 1969 and has been rigorously home-schooling herself ever since. She raised four children, founded and managed a technical writing business, TechProse, and was co-founder of the non-profit, Opportunity Junction, now in its 12th year. Natchez' most recent book is a bilingual volume of translations from the *Russian: Poems From the Stray Dog Café: Akhmatova, Mandelstam* and *Gumilev.* She is co-translator of *Tadeusz Borowski: Selected Poems.* Her book of poems, *Jade Suit,* appeared in 2001. She blogs at www.dactlys-and-drakes.com.

DIANA KHOI NGUYEN, a native of California, is a recipient of awards from the Academy of American Poets and the Key West Literary Seminar. She's also received scholarships from the Bread Loaf Writers Conference and the Fine Arts Work Center in Provincetown. Diana's poems and reviews appear or are forthcoming in *Poetry, The Collagist, Memorious, Lana Turner,* and elsewhere. www.dianakhoinguyen.com

AMY PENCE authored the poetry collections *Armor, Amour* (Ninebark Press, 2012) and *The Decadent Lovely* (Main Street Rag, 2010). Her hybrid work on Emily Dickinson, *[It] Incandescent,* was a finalist for Tupelo Press, the Colorado Prize for Poetry and the Drunken Boat manuscript contest. Poems she wrote at Squaw Valley won first prize in a poetry contest sponsored by Soundings East. She lives with her husband in Carrollton, Georgia; her daughter is off to college.

ANNA ROSS is the author of *If a Storm,* winner of the 2012 Robert Dana-Anhinga Prize for Poetry, and the forthcoming chapbook *Figuring,* a finalist for the 2015 Alice Fay Di Castagnola Award. She has received grants and fellowships from the Massachusetts Cultural Council, Sewanee Writers' Conference, and the Squaw Valley Poetry Workshop, and her poems have appeared or are forthcoming *Barrow Street, Memorious, The Southern Review, Tupelo Quarterly, The Paris Review,* and other journals. She teaches in the Writing, Literature & Publishing Program at Emerson College and is a contributing editor for *Salamander.*

LARRY RUTH neglected to provide a CV or a biography. Here's what we've pieced together: in the third grade, in celebration of a certain winter holiday, he wrote a play about elves on strike, which was performed by his class. After the first performance, in solidarity with the elves, he abandoned the dramatic arts, and earned several degrees at Berkeley. He works in environmental and natural resources policy, and enjoys the remnants of the wild.

PETER SCHIRESON divides his time between Palo Alto and the Sierra Foothills. Retired from a long business career, Peter is ordained as a Zen priest and is one of the teachers at Zen Center of Fresno. His poems have appeared or are forthcoming in *Post Road, New Delta Review, Quiddity, The Lyric,* and other journals.

MEARA SHARMA is an artist, writer, and dancer. She has contributed to the *New York Times, NPR, Deutsche Welle,* Almirah Radio, *Matador,* and elsewhere. She works as a nonfiction editor for *Guernica* magazine, and a producer for the public radio program *On the Media.* She lives in Brooklyn.

EVIE SHOCKLEY is a poet and literary scholar. Her poetry collections include *the new black* (Wesleyan), as well as *a half-red sea* and two chapbooks. She has also published a book of criticism, *Renegade Poetics: Black Aesthetics and Formal Innovation in African American Poetry* (Iowa). She is Associate Professor of English at Rutgers University-New Brunswick, where she teaches African American literature and creative writing. She attended the Poetry Workshop as a participant and has returned as a staff member several times, most recently in 2013.

JACQUELINE HUGHES SIMON: After a long hiatus from poetry she rediscovered her love of the form while attending UC Berkeley as a returning student in 2011. While there she was able to participate in workshops with talented writers Catherine Gallagher, John Shoptaw and Robert Hass. She won the Judith Lee Stronach Poetry Prize for re-entry students in 2013.

KATHI STAFFORD's writing has appeared in *Rattle, Chiron Review, Connecticut River Review,* and numerous other literary journals. She is also a contributing writer to *Portuguese American Journal.* Her poetry has appeared in numerous anthologies, such as *Chopin with Cherries* and *Sea of Alone: Poems for Alfred Hitchcock.* She previously served for several years as Poetry Editor and Senior Editor for *Southern California Review.* Her book of poems, *Blank Check,* will be published in Fall 2015.

CARL STEEN: C.R. Steen was born in New York City and lives in Southern California. He is a past particpant in the Squaw Valley Community of Writers Workshops for Poetry and Fiction. "Helpless" is for Janette Montagano with love.

SHEILA DAVIES SUMNER has an MFA in Poetry from St. Mary's College of California. Her poems have appeared most recently in the online literary journal *Between The Lines* and in the Zine, *Index Fist*. She has also written short stories which appeared in *Rampike*, *Alcatraz 3*, and in the graphic-story magazine, *one of one*, published by Burning Books. In addition, she has written and produced radio dramas commissioned by New American Radio, including "What is the Matter in Amy Glennon," which was nominated for the International Prix Futura Award. Currently, she is co-curator for the Studio One Reading Series in Oakland, California and is writing a book-length collection of poems.

PAUL WATSKY, co-translator of *Santoka* (Tokyo, PIE Books, 2006) and author of the collection *Telling The Difference* (Fisher King Press, 2010), will have a new book out, also from Fisher King, in early 2015. His work has appeared in such journals as *Interim*, *The Carolina Quarterly*, *Word Riot*, *Smartish Pace*, and *Rattle*.

DAVID WATTS has won the Talent House Press award, The Francis Lock Prize for the most imaginative poem, and placed second in the Sunken Garden poetry prize. Two books and five chapbooks of his poetry are published, two CD's of word-jazz, two collections of short stories (Random House and U. Iowa Press) and two anthologies on the subject of literature and healing (U. California Press). He was Executive Producer (along with Joan Baranow) of the PBS Documentary, *Healing Words: Poetry and Medicine*, which aired during 2008-9.

MARTHA YATES is a winner the Barbara Deming Memorial and the Southwest Literary Center Discovery Award and has won numerous academic awards as well. She has graduate degrees in Latin, Greek and the philosophy of religion. Her doctorate is in Classics with a specialty in Early Greek lyric poetry and tragedy. Her poems and essays have appeared in *The Harwood Review*, *Krisis: A Journal of Philosophy*, *Favonius*, and *Sinister Wisdom* and as well as other publications, and her photographs in *The New York Times* and *Print Magazine*. For many years she has worked as an archaeologist and firefighter; public radio station KRZA in Alamosa, Colorado aired an interview with Martha titled: "Archaeologist, Firefighter and Poet."

www.ingramcontent.com/pod-product-compliance
Lightning Source LLC
Chambersburg PA
CBHW032034090426
42741CB00006B/806

* 9 780988 895317 *